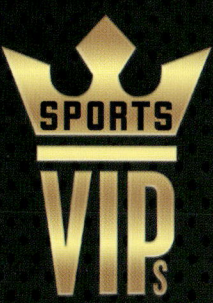

SPORTS
VIPs

MEET
JUSTIN
JEFFERSON

ELLIOTT SMITH

Lerner Publications ◆ Minneapolis

SPORTS THRILLS *MEET* RESEARCH SKILLS

Lerner SPORTS

Free Database Trial: **lernersports.com**

Lerner Publications Company
An imprint of Lerner Publishing Group, Inc.
241 First Avenue North
Minneapolis, MN 55401 USA

For reading levels and more information, look up this title at www.lernerbooks.com.

Main body text set in Aptifer Slab LT Pro. Typeface provided by Linotype AG.

Editor: Matt Doeden

Library of Congress Cataloging-in-Publication Data

Names: Smith, Elliott, 1976– author.
Title: Meet Justin Jefferson : Minnesota Vikings superstar / Elliott Smith.
Description: Minneapolis, MN : Lerner Publications, [2024] | Series: Sports VIPs (Lerner sports) | Includes
    bibliographical references and index. | Audience: Ages 7–11 | Audience: Grades 4–6 | Summary: "Explore the
    life of Justin Jefferson, one of the most exciting wide receivers in the NFL. Jefferson's football skills have made
    him a superstar, and Minnesota Vikings fans love to watch his touchdown dance"— Provided by publisher.
Identifiers: LCCN 2022056400 (print) | LCCN 2022056401 (ebook) | ISBN 9781728490946 (library binding) |
    ISBN 9798765603970 (paperback) | ISBN 9798765601310 (ebook)
Subjects: LCSH: Jefferson, Justin, 1999– —Biography—Juvenile literature. | Wide receivers (Football)—
    Biography—Juvenile literature. | Football players—United States—Biography—Juvenile literature. |
    Minnesota Vikings (Football team)—Juvenile literature. | BISAC: JUVENILE NONFICTION / Biography &
    Autobiography / Sports & Recreation
Classification: LCC GV939.J44 S65 2023 (print) | LCC GV939.J44 (ebook) | DDC 796.332092 [B]—dc23/eng/20221130

LC record available at https://lccn.loc.gov/2022056400
LC ebook record available at https://lccn.loc.gov/2022056401

Manufactured in the United States of America
2-1010603-51043-1/24/2024

TABLE OF CONTENTS

>>>>>>>>>>>>

FOURTH AND LONG

Justin Jefferson and the Minnesota Vikings needed a miracle. On November 13, 2022, the Vikings were locked in a tough battle with the Buffalo Bills. Late in the fourth quarter, the Vikings trailed by four points. On fourth down, the Vikings needed 18 yards to keep their hopes alive.

Minnesota quarterback Kirk Cousins took the snap and dropped back. He threw the ball deep down the sideline toward his wide receiver. Jefferson jumped up and reached his arm in the air. He grabbed the ball with one hand. The Buffalo defensive back grabbed the ball with two hands.

FAST FACTS

DATE OF BIRTH: June 16, 1999

POSITION: wide receiver

LEAGUE: National Football League (NFL)

PROFESSIONAL HIGHLIGHTS: won national championship at Louisiana State University (LSU); named the *Sporting News* Rookie of the Year in 2020; set NFL record for most receiving yards in first two seasons

PERSONAL HIGHLIGHTS: third member of family to play college football at LSU; first NFL player featured in *Fortnite*; designed series of hats for Lids

As Jefferson fell to the ground, he snatched the ball away. He secured the ball as he crashed onto the turf. His teammates were in shock. Many fans and NFL experts called it one of the greatest catches they had ever seen.

The 32-yard catch kept the drive alive. It was one of many amazing plays the star receiver made in the game. He finished with 10 catches for 193 yards as the Vikings

Jefferson (*number 18*) battles Buffalo defender Cam Lewis for the ball on a key fourth-down play on November 13, 2022.

Jefferson tosses the ball to an official after making a catch against the Bills on November 13, 2022.

rallied for an overtime victory, 33–30. The big game proved once again that Jefferson is one of the best players in the NFL.

"It felt like it was unreal. Like a movie," Jefferson said. "The big games, the big moments, when people are looking for you to make a play, that's what I like the most."

CHAPTER 1

OVERLOOKED

Justin Jefferson's story proves that most NFL players aren't born into success. Jefferson was born June 16, 1999, in St. Rose, Louisiana. He had two older brothers, Jordan and Rickey. Both of them were talented athletes. They encouraged their little brother to play sports.

As a boy, Justin carried a football everywhere he went. There was an empty lot next to the Jefferson family's home. That was where Justin and his brothers played countless games of football and basketball. When his brothers weren't around, Justin would spend hours in the yard throwing the ball to himself. He'd throw the ball high in the air and race to catch it.

Jefferson (*right*) shakes hands with his older brother Jordan after a Vikings win in 2022. His father, John, stands next to Jordan.

When Justin reached Destrehan High School, he was small by football standards. At 5 feet 7 inches (1.7 m), he lacked the height that receivers need to challenge defenders for catches. He spent most of his first two years on the sidelines. Before his junior season, he sprouted to 6 feet 1 inch (1.9 m).

In his senior year, Justin showed flashes of greatness. He had 44 catches for 956 yards and nine touchdowns.

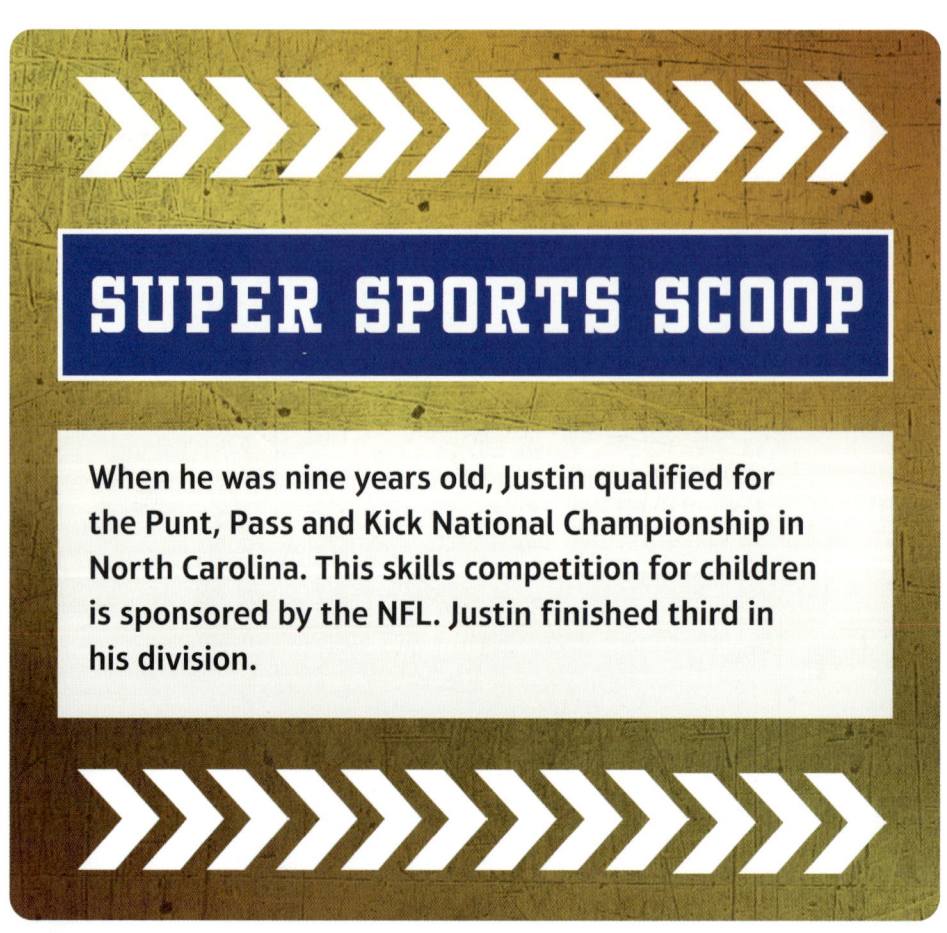

SUPER SPORTS SCOOP

When he was nine years old, Justin qualified for the Punt, Pass and Kick National Championship in North Carolina. This skills competition for children is sponsored by the NFL. Justin finished third in his division.

HOME OF THE FIGHTING WILDCATS

But many college scouts weren't interested in him. He was still short by the standards of college receivers. He also didn't have good enough grades in his English class to graduate. He was a two-star recruit. Many big colleges only go after three- and four-star recruits. One college was always on his radar. Both of Justin's brothers attended LSU. Jordan had been a quarterback for the Tigers. Rickey starred as a defensive back several years later. The love for LSU ran deep in the family.

Jordan Jefferson tosses a pass for LSU in 2008.

Rickey Jefferson intercepts a pass for LSU in a 2014 game against Florida.

LSU promised Justin a scholarship if he improved his grades. He hit the books and earned the grades he needed to graduate. In 2017, Justin received LSU's last remaining scholarship for the upcoming season.

"They stuck to their promise. As an LSU family, we respected that," said Justin's father. "They could've closed that door. [They] made that promise, and that gave Justin motivation."

CHAPTER 2

GROWING STAR

Because Jefferson signed with LSU so late, he missed the first week of training camp. When he arrived, he did not get superstar treatment. Many of his teammates did not realize the quiet receiver had a scholarship. They thought he was a walk-on, which is a player who tries out for the team without any guarantee of making it.

Jefferson quickly made an impact in practice. His talent was clear to the LSU coaches. But he didn't play much his freshman year. Jefferson didn't have a single catch.

His second year was a different story. Jefferson finally got a chance to shine. He led LSU with 54 catches and 875 yards. He also scored six touchdowns. The Tigers were a good team, but not a great one. That would change during Jefferson's junior year.

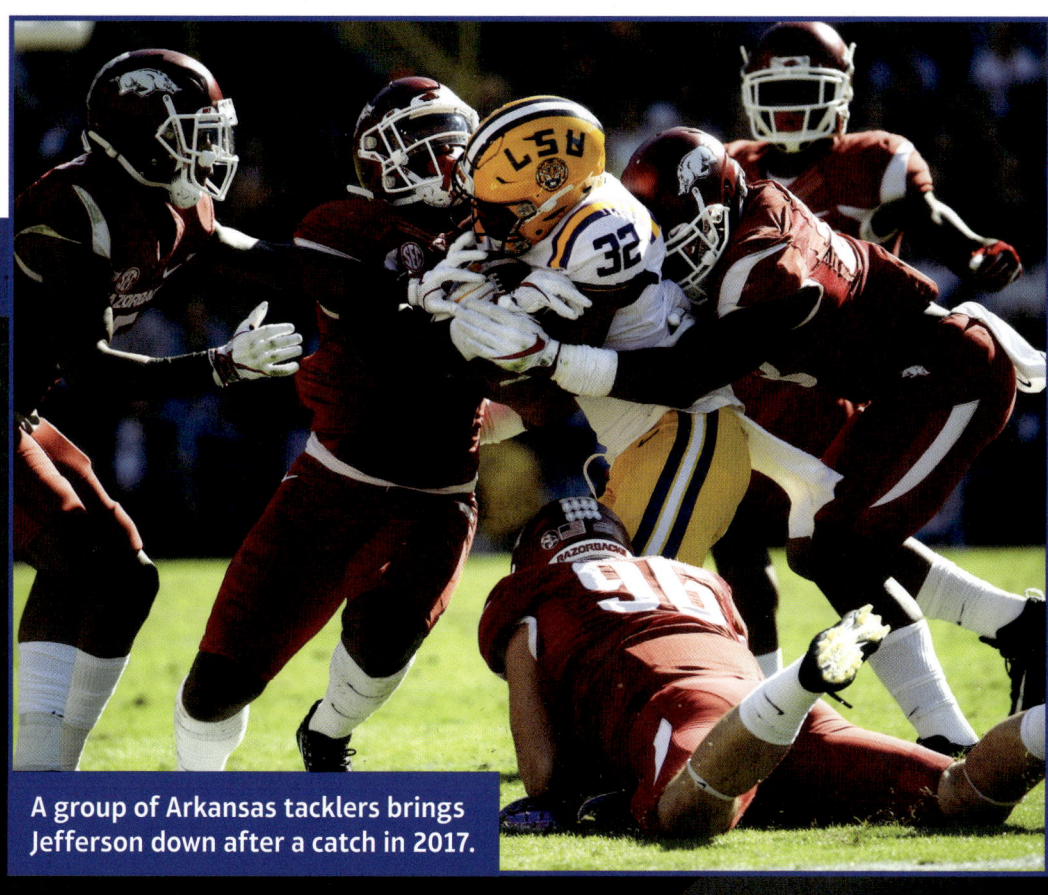

A group of Arkansas tacklers brings Jefferson down after a catch in 2017.

Jefferson reaches out for the goal line at the Peach Bowl in 2019. He scored four touchdowns in the first half of the game. LSU won and advanced to the championship game.

The 2019 LSU team made a couple of changes on offense. Jefferson moved to a new receiver position, the slot. That allowed him to use his speed on inside pass routes. Jefferson also developed a good connection with quarterback Joe Burrow. The results were record-breaking.

Jefferson finished with 111 receptions as a junior. That was the most in college football. He also had 18 touchdowns. That was second to teammate Ja'Marr Chase. Jefferson saved some his best performances for the most important games. He scored four touchdowns in the first half of the Peach Bowl. The Tigers advanced to the College Football Playoff National Championship.

Jefferson had nine catches for 106 yards as LSU beat Clemson, 42–25.

The skinny kid that wasn't on anyone's radar had proved the doubters wrong. LSU went undefeated and won the national championship. Jefferson celebrated with family and friends.

"Definitely the best team ever in college football," he said. "It was definitely a fun year that whole year."

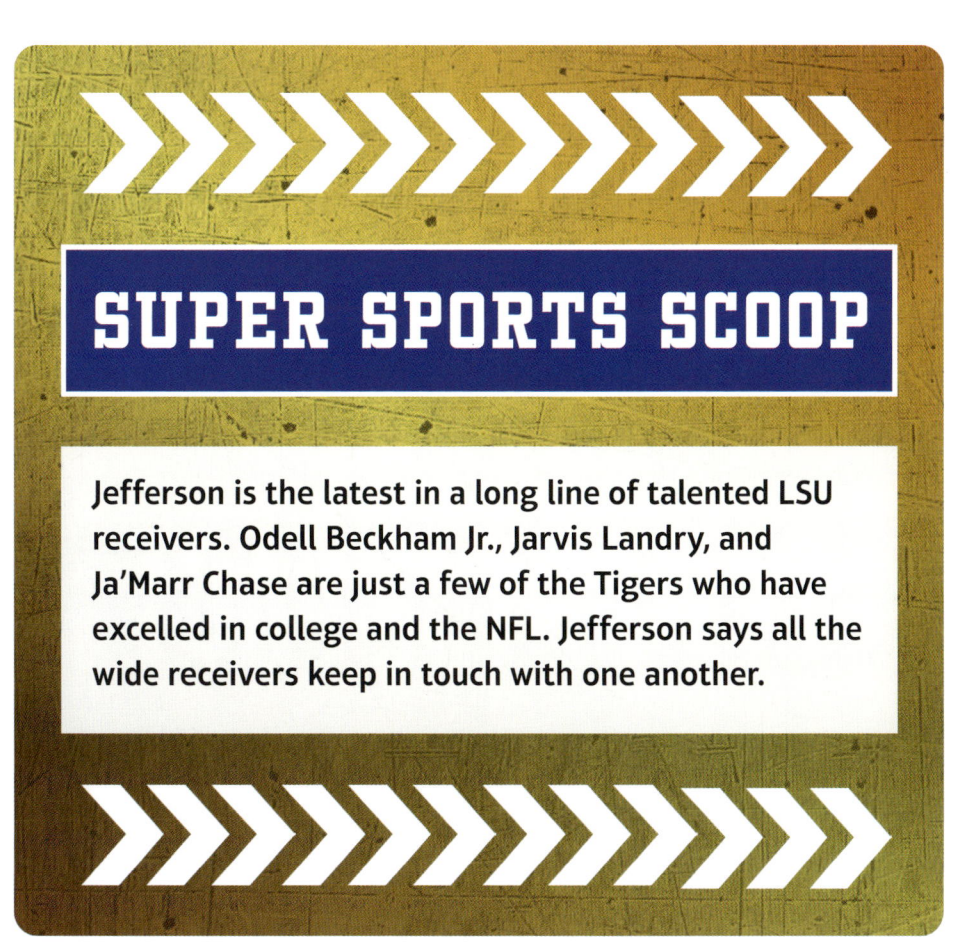

SUPER SPORTS SCOOP

Jefferson is the latest in a long line of talented LSU receivers. Odell Beckham Jr., Jarvis Landry, and Ja'Marr Chase are just a few of the Tigers who have excelled in college and the NFL. Jefferson says all the wide receivers keep in touch with one another.

CHAPTER 3

INSTANT IMPACT

After his junior season, Jefferson was ready for a new challenge. He entered the 2020 NFL Draft. Once again, the speedy receiver was overlooked. He wasn't even the highest-rated receiver in the draft.

On April 23, 2020, Jefferson watched as teams made pick after pick. Four receivers were selected before Jefferson. Finally, the Minnesota Vikings chose Jefferson with the twenty-second pick.

Jefferson runs after making a catch against the Detroit Lions on December 5, 2021.

Jefferson does his Griddy celebration after scoring a 71-yard touchdown against the Tennessee Titans in 2020.

"I tried not to worry about it too much, but it got to me a little bit," Jefferson admitted. "I didn't feel like I was the fifth best receiver in the draft. I just used that as determination, I used that as fuel to keep improving my game."

It didn't take long for Jefferson to prove his worth. In just his third NFL game, he had seven catches for 175 yards against the Tennessee Titans. His first NFL touchdown came on a 71-yard pass. He sped past one defender and faked out a would-be tackler on his way to the end zone.

Jefferson's rookie season was filled with big moments. He had seven games in which he had at least 100 receiving yards. Jefferson finished with 88 catches and 1,400 yards. That set the NFL record for rookie receiving yards. He was named Rookie of the Year by the *Sporting News*.

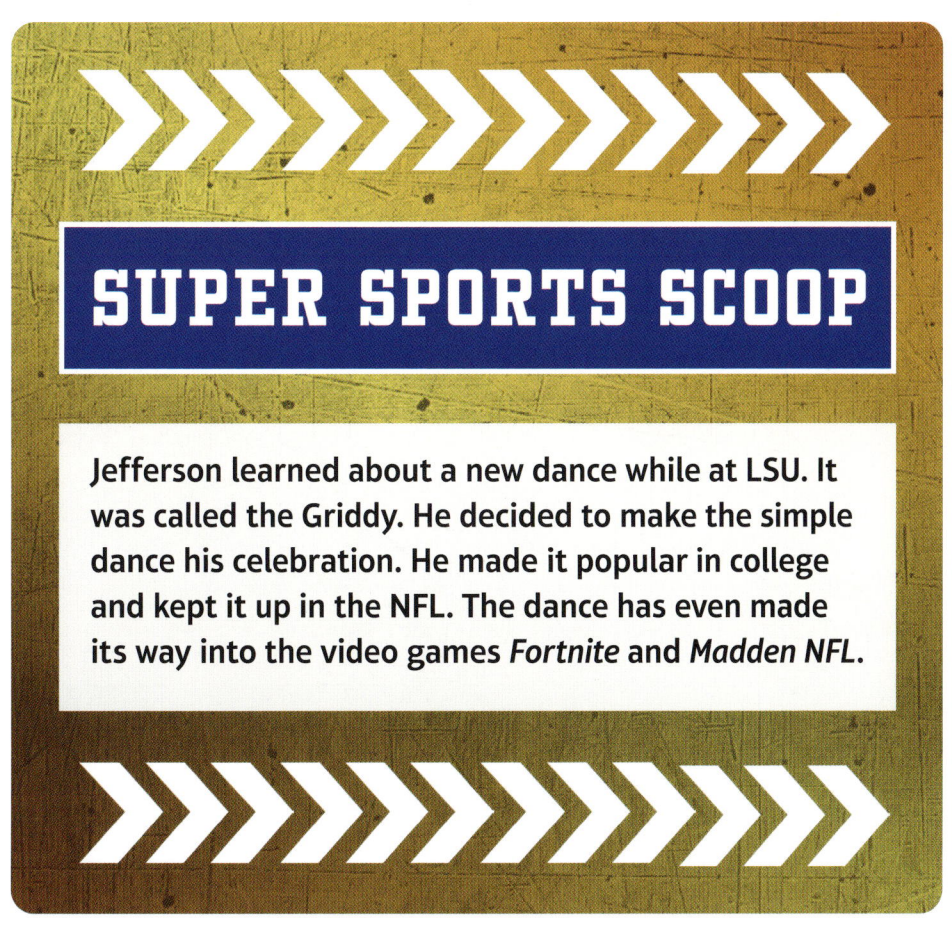

SUPER SPORTS SCOOP

Jefferson learned about a new dance while at LSU. It was called the Griddy. He decided to make the simple dance his celebration. He made it popular in college and kept it up in the NFL. The dance has even made its way into the video games *Fortnite* and *Madden NFL*.

The young superstar picked up where he left off in his second season. In a four-game stretch, Jefferson racked up an amazing 577 yards. His final numbers were eye-popping. He tallied 108 receptions for 1,616 yards. Jefferson set an NFL record for most receiving yards in a player's first two seasons. Jefferson had already become one of the league's most feared wide receivers.

Jefferson tries to elude a Detroit Lions tackler in 2021.

CHAPTER 4

BIGGER AND BETTER

Jefferson enjoyed his early success. But he continued to
work on getting better. Before the 2022 season, he said
that his goal was to be the best wide receiver in the NFL.

Jefferson starts the 2022 season with a bang against the Green Bay Packers. Jefferson racked up 184 yards and two touchdowns in the Minnesota victory.

Even though Jefferson entered the season at just 23 years old, he played like a veteran. In the first game of 2022, he put NFL defenses on high alert. Jefferson made 11 catches for 184 yards and two touchdowns in a win over the Green Bay Packers. Through the first nine games of 2022, Jefferson already had more than 1,000 receiving yards. At times he seemed almost impossible to cover.

What makes Jefferson so tough for defenses to stop? He has all the tools. He's fast. He runs excellent routes, which means his quarterback always knows exactly where he will be. His strong hands and his leaping ability give him the chance to bring in even difficult passes.

"One of the traits that makes Justin special is when the ball goes up in the air, he plays in such a way where he says, 'That's my football,'" Vikings quarterback

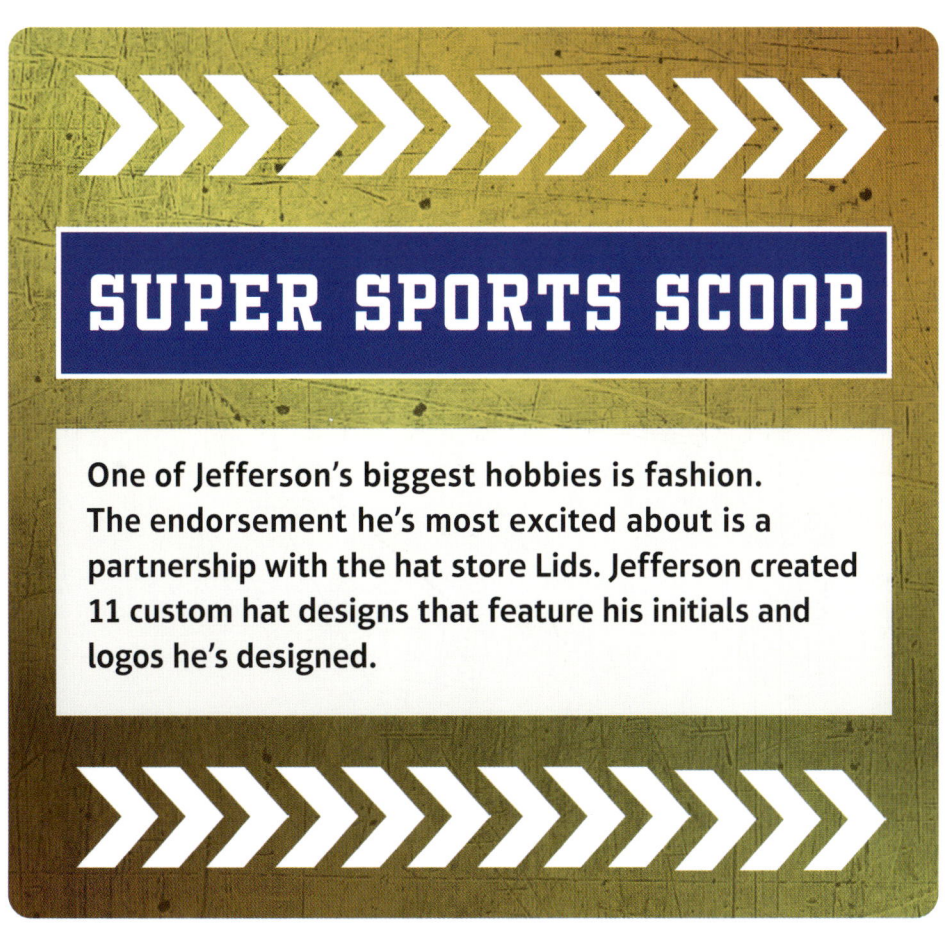

SUPER SPORTS SCOOP

One of Jefferson's biggest hobbies is fashion. The endorsement he's most excited about is a partnership with the hat store Lids. Jefferson created 11 custom hat designs that feature his initials and logos he's designed.

Jefferson makes a leaping catch for a touchdown in a Minnesota victory over the Washington Commanders in 2022.

Jefferson (*left*) gives a high five to his quarterback, Kirk Cousins, during a 2022 practice.

Kirk Cousins said. The future is very bright for Jefferson. After the 2022 season, the receiver is in line for a new contract. Many experts believe it could be a record-breaking salary.

But Jefferson has other goals in mind. One is helping the Vikings make the playoffs and win the Super Bowl. And he hasn't forgotten his goal to be the best receiver in the league. As he continues to pile up big numbers and amazing catches, it gets harder and harder to argue against the two-star recruit.

JUSTIN JEFFERSON CAREER STATS

GAMES PLAYED:
50

CATCHES:
324

RECEIVING YARDS:
4,825

YARDS PER CATCH:
14.9

LONGEST CATCH:
71 YARDS

TOUCHDOWNS:
26

Stats are accurate through the 2022 NFL season.

GLOSSARY

draft: when teams take turns choosing new players

reception: a catch made by an offensive player

recruit: a newcomer to an activity

rookie: a first-year player

route: the planned path that a receiver takes down the field

scholarship: money given to a student to help pay for their education

scout: someone who judges prospects to predict how successful they might be at the next level of a sport

slot: an inside wide receiver position that often focuses on catches over the middle of the field

veteran: an experienced player

walk-on: a player who tries out for a sport without being recruited or having a scholarship

SOURCE NOTES

7   John Wawrow, "Sunday Stunner: Vikings Take Advantage Of Critical Allen Turnovers, Beat Bills In OT," Jamestown (NY) *Post-Journal*, November 14, 2022, https://www.post-journal.com /sports/local-sports/2022/11/sunday-stunner/.

13 Brooks Kubena, "LSU Family Legacy Continues through Justin Jefferson: 'It's like He Was Destined to Do It,'" *Advocate*, September 20, 2018, https://www.theadvocate.com/baton_rouge /sports/lsu/article_415c10de-bd26-11e8-9f4f-e3944215315b.html.

17 Kameron Hay, "Justin Jefferson Says Davante Adams Is the Best Wide Receiver for Now," *Complex*, July 14, 2022, https:// www.complex.com/sports/justin-jefferson-best-wide-receiver.

20 Tyler R. Tynes, "What Justin Jefferson Learned in His First Season in Minnesota," *GQ*, April 21, 2021, https://www.gq.com /story/justin-jefferson-first-season-minnesota.

25 Jon Krawczynski, "Kirk Cousins' Trust in Justin Jefferson Makes Vikings More Dangerous Than Ever," Athletic, October 31, 2022, https://theathletic.com/3745024/2022/10/31 /kirk-cousins-justin-jefferson-vikings/.

LEARN MORE

Anderson, Josh. *Minnesota Vikings*. Mankato, MN: Child's World, 2022.

Fishman, Jon M. *Joe Burrow*. Minneapolis: Lerner Publications, 2022.

Hewson, Anthony K. *Odell Beckham Jr*. Minneapolis: Lerner Publications, 2020.

Kiddle: National Football League Facts for Kids
https://kids.kiddle.co/National_Football_League

Minnesota Vikings
https://www.vikings.com

Sports Illustrated Kids: Football
https://www.sikids.com/football

INDEX

PHOTO ACKNOWLEDGMENTS

Image credits: Isaiah Vazquez/Getty Images, pp. 4, 6, 7; AP Photo/Michael
Conroy, p. 8; AP Photo/Gerald Herbert, p. 9; Spatms/Wikipedia commons,
p. 11; Wesley Hitt/Getty Images, pp. 12, 14; Rob Foldy/Getty Images, p. 13;
Chris Graythen/Getty Images, p. 15; Todd Kirkland/Getty Images, p. 16;
Alika Jenner/Getty Images, p. 18; Gregory Shamus/Getty Images, pp. 19,
22; AP Photo/Elizabeth Flores/Star Tribune, p. 20; David Berding/Getty
Images, pp. 23, 27; Stephen Maturen/Getty Images, p. 24; AP Photo/Daniel
Kucin Jr., p. 26.

Cover: Cal Sport Media/Alamy Stock Photo.